Master Getting Things Done the David Allen Way with Evernote

Your 7-Day GTD Immediate Action Plan

Dominic Wolff

ORGANIZED LIVING
P R E S S

Atlanta, Georgia USA

ISBN 978-1-49101-030-3

9 781491 010303 >

EDITORIAL REVIEWS

Thank you for downloading my book. Please REVIEW this book on Amazon. I need your feedback to make the next version better. Thank you so much!

BOOKS BY DOMINIC WOLFF

Getting Things Done (GTD) + Evernote = Ultimate Productivity

Total Time Mastery with Evernote

Your Killer Linkedin Profile

Building Connections 2014

IS THIS BOOK FOR YOU

Life is not like a walk in the park, that's for sure, and it's definitely not a box of chocolates, that's sweet but unreal; life is hard, and as time goes by it becomes even harder for some people as they grow older, their anxiety levels rise, and their everyday routines seem to suck their years away.

I have written this book to help people like these; people who feel that they've reached a dead end, who are down, who have lost all energy and abandoned their dreams for a better future. Fear not, I'm not a guru. I'm just somebody who once found myself in a very bad place, and decided that I would do whatever I possibly could to survive, and if possible, improve my life.

As you'll easily come to understand by reading my book my journey was not that painful. Yes, it did require some sacrifices but they were sacrifices that I was willing to make. I started by killing my habits, then I changed my routines, and I finished by learning new tricks, tricks that would lead me to a better place. I'm certain that what worked for me can work for you as well, and as a result you'll manage to kill your demons and live a long and successful life.

TABLE OF CONTENTS

Author's introduction

If there's one thing that just about everyone can agree on, it's that we're busy. Very busy. Between added responsibilities at work, taking care of a house, managing finances, and maybe keeping your family running, you have a lot to do. And while we become more technologically advanced and have more ways to organize and access information, we continue to get busier. This is why David Allen published *Getting Things Done* in 2001. Since its publication, the book has gained a huge following, with very committed adherents, many of whom say that it's changed their life (if you're not sure what the book is about, keep reading and you'll find out). The first part of this book will get you acquainted with the ideas of GTD, the system that's outlined in Allen's book. The second part of the book will show you how to implement the system using Evernote, a free application for Windows, Mac, and mobile. This is a very powerful tool with which to organize your life (let's face it; though the methods outlined in Allen's book are fantastic, they're a bit behind the times).

I can tell you from personal experience that setting up, committing to, and sticking with this system will make a big change in your life (or, at least, your organizational and productive life . . . which is likely your work life). I've always been a bit of an overachiever and as a graduate student I was taking more than a full-course load while actively participating in multiple student organizations. Needless to say, I eventually became overwhelmed. I knew there just had to be a better way than constantly pulling all-nighters and developing a solid caffeine habit. And thus, my deep love affair with personal management systems began. A love affair that's spanned almost two decades, resulting in a career in organizational development and personal productivity management with a master's degree in the works.

By using the tools and strategies that I present in this book, you'll get everything that you need to remember or do out of your head and into your computer, where it can be categorized, managed, and efficiently tracked, which will free up your mind and give you some much needed mental space.

. The experience of having your priorities, responsibilities, and tasks organized in this way is extremely liberating, and after you implement and begin to trust the system, you'll feel a weight lifting from you; you can fight stress and inefficiency at the same time!

The key to getting to this point is using technology in a way that's helpful, instead of just more stressful. Most people I know get an absolutely baffling amount of e-mail every day, and are almost constantly on their smartphones looking things up, sending text messages, and coordinating various things. You've heard it dozens of times before—technology is supposed to make our lives easier, not busier! Well, welcome to the first step in making technology work *for* you, instead of *against* you. I hope you enjoy this book, and I hope that you find the system I outline to be useful in getting your life back under control. I sincerely believe that with a bit of time and a healthy dose of commitment, this can make a big difference in your life.

Good luck!

—Dominic Wolff

1. What You'll Need

This book is about getting yourself, your workflow, and your life organized with GTD and Evernote. Fortunately, you don't need much to do this! However, there is a short list of things that you'll want to make sure you have to get started.

1. A computer (desktop or laptop).
2. A mobile device (smartphone or tablet; this is optional, but recommended).
3. Evernote (we'll go over downloading this in chapter 4.1).
4. A scanner (this can be as simple as a camera phone or as complex as a full desktop scanner).
5. A physical inbox (this can be a simple wire in-tray or something more substantial; I prefer the simpler styles).
6. A trash can (yes, really).
7. A filing cabinet.
8. A good number of folders and hanging files.
9. A labeller (David Allen recommends the Brother labeller, but you can use any one that you want).*

10. A serious commitment to the project.
11. Several hours (we'll discuss the time commitment in a moment).

* This guide will help you combine the full-digital strategy recommended by the crew at Evernote and the more paper-based style propounded by David Allen. If you're planning on going all-digital, you might not need the labeller, as you'll end up with very few paper materials in your system.

The list above will cover everything in this book up to the penultimate chapter, Super-Advanced Tips, which offers suggestions on using additional websites, and pieces of software and hardware to help you get GTD up and running. These are by no means necessary, but if you're like me, and you find organizing and processing to be almost obscenely satisfying and downright enjoyable (yes, I know, some people might find this idea absolutely horrifying), you might want to consider adding a little bit of complexity for more payoff.

2. GTD Basics

2.1. Everyone's Goal: Getting Things Done

If you're reading this book, I assume that you're already at least somewhat overwhelmed with your to-do list, your calendar, or your project management system; possibly all three. If so, you're not alone. "I'm not getting enough done" is an extremely common refrain among folks from all walks of life, whether they're professionals, students, stay-at-home parents, business owners—or anyone else for that matter. Our society places a huge amount of value on being highly productive and getting a huge amount of things done all the time (whether or not this emphasis is good or not is a topic for another book), and we feel that pressure constantly, which is a huge source of stress for a lot of people. There's no way that we can be productive every hour of our lives— it's just not possible. But we *can* put systems in place to make sure that our productive hours are more efficient, more effective, and more valuable.

This is the point of personal management systems, which are the focus of my work. By helping people get organized, I help them become significantly more efficient, making them more productive with a smaller investment of time. You wouldn't believe how much stress this relieves! When you're well-organized and you use good planning practices, you won't have to keep tons of extra information in the back of your mind, where it takes up space and often gets forgotten. This is the principle behind Getting Things Done (henceforth, GTD), the personal management system created and popularized by David Allen, a productivity consultant. By using this system, you'll stay better organized, you'll be more effective in your project plans, and you'll *get more done*. That's why you're reading this book, isn't it? To learn how to get more done.

One of the main reasons that I'm writing this book in this specific format is because some people are so busy and their schedules are so hectic that they don't have time to read Allen's GTD book. It's a good book, but, to be honest, it's way more than you need. This book will give you an overview of GTD, but will focus on the implementation of the system in your personal situation using Evernote, one of the best (if not the absolute best) applications that can be used for managing your life. But before we get into the implementation process, it's important to understand exactly what GTD is and how it works.

2.2. What is GTD?

This is likely a question that you're going to get quite a bit if you explain to anyone what you're doing (and you'll probably want to after you see how effective it is!). There are quite a few answers, but I think one point that David Allen makes in his book sums up the purpose of the entire system very well: it's a method of getting everything that you need to do out of your head and onto paper (or, in our case, into an electronic format). That's really what it comes down to. Once you go through this process, you'll be absolutely amazed at how many things you're trying to keep track of in your memory right now, and keeping all of these things in memory is hard. It takes effort, it's not very effective, and it can be extremely frustrating, because humans have a tendency to forget things. Even if you think you have a great memory for things that you have to get done, you likely forget a few of them on occasion. If you implement GTD, commit to using it, and do it well, you'll find that you forget almost nothing! It's absolutely amazing what GTD can do for you.

If you want a more complex definition, I'll provide that here. GTD is a workflow process, and Allen defines that process as having five steps:

1. Collecting things that command our attention.
2. Processing what those things mean and what we need to do about them.
3. Organize the results.
4. Review options for what we might do and decide the best course of action.
5. Do it.

Even if you don't have a personal management system right now, your desk is unconscionably cluttered, and you have no idea what's on your schedule, you do these things already, which makes GTD very easy to learn. There's actually very little to learn, in fact—GTD just provides you with a system for best completing each of these steps, ensuring that no item falls through the cracks or gets stuck in the middle of the process.

2.3. How Does GTD Work?

As you can see in the diagram below, GTD is essentially based on a short list of questions that need to be answered, and actions that can be taken based on each of the answers.

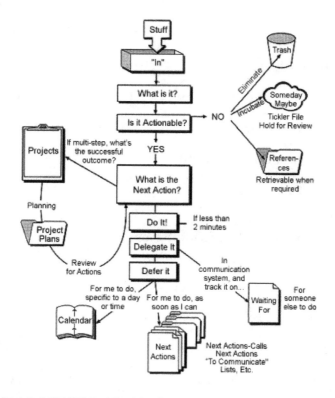

Every item that crosses your desk (be that a very large

oak desk in a corner office, your kitchen table, or your dorm desk) must go through this workflow process, and these questions must be answered. And based on those answers, each item gets placed into a specific container. What happens from there depends on which container the object is in. We'll go over each step one at a time. There are eight containers, each of which I will explain below before continuing on to the rest of the diagram. Before going on to the containers, however, I want to lay out three points that I feel sum up the main points of GTD. These are rules that cannot be broken if the system is going to work (I realize, of course, that sometimes you'll have to break the rules, but if this becomes a habit, you're going to end up back where you started).

1. Establish clear boundaries.

Below, I list eight containers that hold items. These containers must be discrete—if an item is teetering between two different containers, it's likely to get stuck there. And if you create a new container for things that you're not too sure about, that container will become a black hole, with things going in and never coming back out. During the processing phase, you'll need to commit to a location for each item. I can't overstate the importance of this.

2. Follow the actionable rule.

You'll see later that actions related to items in the system are taken in a specific way. Stick with this method; don't switch it up day-to-day. You may think that you have a better idea of what will work well for you, but trust me on this one: follow the system exactly as it's set out for a month. If, after a month, the system has become well-established, but you feel that it could still be made better, then you can experiment with some new things. But until then, just stick to the rules.

3. Obey the calendar.

The calendar is the law—period. If it's on your calendar for today, it gets done today. That's just how it has to be. That probably sounds unreasonably difficult right now, but you'll find that once you get everything organized, nothing will be on your calendar except the things that really need to get done, and done today. This helps you place full confidence in your calendar, because you'll know that you don't have anything that's not important on there. You'll also be able to trust that all of your time-sensitive items are on your calendar. This, too, can be difficult at first, but it pays off in the long run, and it gets a whole lot easier very quickly.

Okay, on to the containers for items in the GTD system.

1. Projects

This is actually a larger category than it sounds. Every item, no matter how large, goes into this container *if it involves more than one action step*. For example, if you're organizing a dinner with some friends, you'll have to call those friends, plan the meal, and buy groceries. That's three steps, making "dinner with friends" an item that goes on your projects list. It's a bit strange using these criteria for a container called Projects, but you'll get the hang of it pretty quickly.

2. Project Support Materials.

Some people call this "Project Plans," but the idea is the same: everything related to your projects stays here. The Projects container discussed above is just a list—it doesn't include the brochure from the photographer that you're going to hire for the company picnic (you can see the difference between lists and files in the diagram above). That stays in the Project Support Materials file. Allen recommends keeping this out of sight, and I think this is a very good idea. Keep it close at hand, so you can reference it whenever you need to, but if you can see this at all times, you're likely to get distracted during the day.

3. Calendar.

This is a central storage place in GTD. Every action that's time-specific (like appointments) or day-specific (time-sensitive to-do items), and every piece of day-specific information (useful information for a certain day), goes on the calendar. No exceptions. This is crucial for establishing trust in your calendar, which will go a long way toward relieving your stress by emptying your mind of all of the things it's currently storing. If your calendar doesn't contain absolutely everything that you need to do, the system won't work.

4. Next Action lists.

This is the list that you'll likely go to whenever you have some free time during the day and want to get something done. If you can't complete an item immediately, it'll go here so that you can come back to it later. Notice that this is called Next Action *lists*, and not just "list." This is so you can keep separate lists for different types or categories of actions. For example, if you have a lot of calls to make and e-mails to send, you might have a Calls list and an E-mails list. If you're a working student, you could have a Professional and an Academic list. If you have a family, you might have Husband / Wife, Kids, Home, Work, School . . . you can use whatever you like, as long as it helps you stay organized.

5. "Waiting For" list.

One thing that you'll see later is that to be fully effective in GTD, you'll have to learn to delegate things that are better handled by others. This is something that takes practice, but it's worth doing because it'll help you save a lot of time in the long run. And because everyone will be handling the things that they're best equipped to handle, learning to delegate will make your entire workgroup more efficient. Once you delegate something, it goes on this list so that you're reminded that you're waiting for its completion, though it's not on your Projects list—it's on someone else's.

6. Someday list.

This is a list that contains things that can't be acted on immediately or in the very near future. For example, if you want to remember to call your accountant on February 20 to start preparing to file your taxes, but it's only November, that will go on this list. Or if you want to look into tickets for this year's baseball playoffs, but your team hasn't made the cut quite yet, you can put an item here to remind you to take another look when the standings are solidified. Things that you're not quite sure you're going to do can also go here. Things like "take a cooking class," "build a wine rack," "buy a second car," or anything else that you aspire to, but aren't absolutely sure that you're going to get to. You can have subcategories here, too, like "Books I want to read," "Albums I want to buy," or "Things I want to learn to do." These are things that you'll be reminded of on a regular basis, so it's still an important list—items don't go here to die. They're just warming the benches, as it were.

7. Reference Material.

This is one of the areas that many people had never really thought about, but find extremely useful. This is a storage place for all sorts of items that don't require any action. For example, if you kept a bus map from the last time you were in Chicago, and you think you might find it useful when you go back next year, this is where you'll keep it. Reference material should be divided into categories—the "Chicago" category, for example. "Wedding plans," "fishing," "product manuals," and "past taxes" can all go in here, and they'll be safely kept in a location where you can find them without trouble.

8. Trash.

This is a very important container, and it's likely one that you'll be using a whole lot during the early stages of getting organized. Having a trash bin (a physical one) right next to your desk is crucial—if you don't have one, you might begin to let trash pile up on your desk, obscuring other important items and derailing the system.

In Allen's *Getting Things Done*, these were all physical files and locations. However, with our increased reliance on electronic materials, almost everything that you get will be in an electronic form, meaning that all (or nearly all) of these containers can be kept on your computer, which is even more convenient, because you can have access to them whenever you want, wherever you are. I find that some of these can be split between the two, like Reference Material— if I want to keep the brochure for the next race that I'm running, I'll need a physical file, but most things can go into the electronic one.

Now that you understand the containers, I'll move onto the actual workflow. Moving things through this workflow is called "processing," and I'll be referring back to it a lot throughout the rest of this book. It begins with "Stuff," which is all of the things that are in your head and on your desk. This goes to your "In" box, which, again, can be split between an electronic and a physical location. Everything in your inbox then goes through the following workflow, one item at a time. It's good to get in the habit of getting a single item all the way through the workflow before moving onto the next one. If something gets stuck in the middle, it can be awfully hard to get it moving again.

Step 1: What is it?

This step might seem superfluous, but it's actually quite important. One reason that things start to pile up is that we don't *really* know what they are. Say you get an envelope from your power company, and you open it and see a paper jam-packed with small print. What is it? Is it a bill? A notice of a change in your plan? A questionnaire? A simple account statement? If you don't know, you're reasonably likely to just toss it on your desk and tell yourself that you'll deal with it later. However, if you find out exactly what this document is, you can do something about it. This is true with everything, whether it's a piece of mail, an e-mail from a colleague, a note from your boss, a voicemail, or anything else. When something enters the system, you have to know what it is before you can progress.

Step 2: Is it actionable?

What this question comes down to is whether or not something has to be done to resolve whatever it is we're looking at. Let's say that letter from the power company is just a notice on some legislation that was passed in your state. There's nothing that needs to be done, so the answer to this question is "no." But what if it's a statement that you underpaid your last bill by a few dollars? Then the answer is "yes," because something needs to be done about it.

Step 2a: Not actionable.

If the answer in step 2 is "no," then you have three options. First, you can get rid of the item by putting it in the trash. If there's no action that you can take on it now, and there's no action that needs to be taken later, and you don't think you'll find this item useful in the future, the trash is likely where it belongs. If you think that action can or should be taken later, but you're not sure when that is, or you're not sure if you're going to take that action, it can go on your Someday list. If you decide that you'd like to sign up for the cooking class you received an advertisement for, but you're not sure when would be a good time to do that, you can put that item on your Someday list (on a personal note, I like to keep this list relatively sparse, lest it get overwhelming). And if it's something that's not actionable, but you'd like to keep it on hand, then it goes into your general reference material file. This is a good place for things like e-mails about new restaurants in your area, a guide to your city, information on a project at work, and things like that. You want to have access to them in the future, but you don't want them cluttering up your desk.

Step 2b: Actionable.

If the item you're processing is actionable, it gets moved along the pipeline to step 3.

Step 3: What's the next step?

Allen comes back to "next actions" over and over in

his book—understanding what the next step is in processing an item is crucial for moving along through the system efficiently. Using the above example, let's say that the document from your power company is a notice of a change in your plan: your rate's going up. If you decide that you'd like to do something about this, like change power companies, then this is an actionable item.

Changing providers is a multi-step process, so a new project will be created: "Find new power provider." What's the next action? "Research power rates from area providers," or maybe "Ask friends for power provider recommendations." Make a list of actions that need to be taken and keep them on your Projects list in a sub-list under Find new power provider. You can then file the letter in your Project Support Materials so that you always have it on hand for when you decide to start taking on this project.

Step 4: The two-minute rule.

Allen is big on the two-minute rule. During the processing phase (when you'll be moving things along in the workflow), you should only be stopping to take actions if something can be done in two minutes or less. This prevents you from getting side-tracked and losing your place in the process. If an item can't be done in two minutes, but still needs to be done, it will be deferred and end up in one of two containers.

If the item has a clear-cut deadline, and has to be done on a certain day, it goes to the calendar. Make a note in your desk calendar or create an event in your electronic calendar with the name of the task and any quick notes you'd like to jot down about it (in less than two minutes). By putting it on your calendar, you guarantee that you won't forget about it, and that it will be done in a timely fashion.

If there isn't a clear-cut deadline, and you just want to get the item done as soon as you can, it goes to a Next Actions list to be dealt with whenever you have some free time.

Now, I know it can be tempting to defer a lot of things, especially if you haven't done step 1 or 2 very well. However, this is the road to disaster. Make absolutely sure you understand what you're dealing with and what needs to happen before deferring something for later.

Step 5: Do or delegate?

These are the final two options for things that can be dealt with in under two minutes. If something that comes across your desk can be done in two minutes or less, do it immediately. Shoot off a quick reply to an e-mail. Sign a form and drop it in your outbox. These are things you can do right away.

However, when processing items, you should always be asking yourself if you're the best person to take care of it. Is someone else better equipped or better prepared to handle it? You'd be surprised at how often you can delegate tasks, and how willing many people are to help you out with them, especially if they're the best person for the job. If everyone in your company did, deferred, or delegated everything that came across their desk, you'd have a productivity machine that could not be rivalled, because everyone would only be taking care of the things that they're best equipped to do.

It's often pretty easy to delegate something in two minutes (for example, by forwarding an e-mail and asking someone to take care of the things discussed in it), but if it's going to take longer, it can go on your Next Actions list.

The three sections above should give you an idea of how GTD works. Of course, there are more details that you can add, and more processes that you can refine, but these are the core principles that define the system. (If you want more details on different parts of the system, I encourage you to read Allen's book.) Once you understand how it's all going to work, you can begin setting up the "infrastructure" for the system so that you'll be able to accomplish all of these steps easily and quickly. We'll begin this in the next chapter.

2.4. The Daily Schedule

Now that the system has been laid out, I'll recommend a way

to use it. Of course, this isn't the only way that it can be done, but this is a good way to start. Every day, the first thing you should do is check either your calendar or your inbox, depending on how you like to work. Personally, I find that I'm better at accomplishing tasks in the morning, so I go straight to the calendar to find out what needs to be done. I do those things first, then I go to my inboxes (physical and electronic) to process everything there. I then look over my Projects and Next Actions lists to see what I can do during the next several hours that would be most helpful.

You may find that a different order works—if you're more motivated in the afternoon, for example, you may want to process the items in your inboxes first. Or look at your "Waiting For" list to see who you might have to follow up with that day. It mostly depends on your working style. Whatever works best for you, stick with—once you develop a routine, you'll become even more efficient.

2.5. The First Day (or Weekend)

Hopefully you see why this workflow is so effective—there's no room for anything to get lost, and there are clear, concrete questions and answers that drive items through the process. However, before all of the things in your mind and on your desk can be processed and placed in the right containers, they all have to make it into your inbox. This is a crucial step in the setup of GTD. In his book, David Allen recommends setting aside a day to do this—don't answer the phone, don't check your e-mail, clear your calendar—though some people might need an entire weekend. Either way, here's what you'll have to do.

1. Get every physical item on your desk into an "In" tray.
2. Perform a "brain dump" to get as many of the things that are currently in your head into your inbox as well. (This will be discussed in more detail in section 4.3.)
3. Begin processing every item that's now in your inbox.

I know this might sound extremely difficult, and I'm going to be honest with you—it can be at times. But it's definitely worth the time that it takes, and you'll be really glad that you did it!

Once all of the "Stuff" that you're working with is in

your inboxes, you're ready to start.

2.6. Is it really effective?

There's a lot of debate over which personal management systems and styles are the most effective. Personally, I believe that there are as many effective styles as there are people. However, I think GTD is, in general, a great place to start, and allows a lot of personalization once you've gotten it set up and running. My personal productivity system looks a lot like GTD, but has been simplified in some areas and more complex in others. Ultimately, it depends on exactly what you want to get out of your personal management system and the resources you're willing to throw at it. For example, I was willing to put loads of time into my system while I was a student, because I knew that without an effective system, I'd never make it through graduate school with my sanity intact (not that there was a great chance of keeping it *anyway*...). Allen's book is full of stories about people who saved hours and hours of work every day because of the system, and people who got their lives back under control by using GTD. It's not a life-changing thing for most people, but I can tell you from experience that a lot of people find that it's a huge help. Give it a shot and see for yourself!

3. Evernote 101

3.1. The basics

Now that you understand how GTD works, it's time to learn about Evernote, one of the most effective and efficient ways to implement the system. If you're like me, you'll soon be using Evernote to keep track of just about everything in your life—I've been using it for years, and I still find new uses for it all the time. It's a wonderful program, and if you need to get yourself together and organized, I think you'll find it absolutely invaluable. In this section, I'll provide the basics of the program, and then I'll go onto some of the features of each version of it. After that, we'll go over getting it set up and getting the GTD system in place.

What is Evernote?

We'll start with the most basic question. Evernote, at its core, is a note-taking and -organizing application for Mac, Windows, iOS, and Android. There's also a web app that you can access from anywhere, which can be extremely valuable if you need to check some of your notes when you don't have one of your devices with you (rare as this may be). At the end of the day, Evernote consists of a simple text editor and a filing system. This might not sound like it's quite as life-changing as I make it sound, but stick with me here and you'll see why I like it so much. The first reason is that your personal copy of the software is connected to your online account, meaning that all of your notes are kept synchronized across all of your devices—if you create or edit a note on your phone, it'll show up on your tablet and your home computer almost instantaneously. This allows you to always have access to your documents, no matter where you are. And if you're somewhere without internet access (on a long train ride, for example), you can use Evernote in the offline mode (if you're a premium subscriber), and it'll sync up when you get connected again.

What can I do with Evernote?

This is a question with a potentially very long answer. Of course, there's personal management. But this only scratches the surface—there are a huge number of people who have given testimonials about using Evernote to run their business or home, innumerable students who use it to take and organize notes, and certainly more than a few people who use it as a kind of catch-all, like the digital equivalent of a junk drawer. Personally, I use it for a combination of these things. You can share notes with others, making it a great collaborative tool. You can add reminders to notes (a relatively recent addition to the functionality of the application), and use it as a calendar or a to-do list. You can use it to plan and keep track of a budget, or your grocery lists, or to manage a reading list. Honestly, I've found there's very little that you *can't* do with Evernote, and this list gets smaller all the time as more functionality gets added, and new functions are being added all the time.

Syncing security

I know that you might be a little hesitant to use the online features of Evernote; you might not feel comfortable with having everything you use to keep your life organized stored on a server somewhere. However, some of the founders of Evernote have a background in digital security, so you can trust them to keep your things safe. Your online data is encrypted, you can encrypt text within notes, and all of the data that's transferred between your computer and your online account is moved securely. You can also now use two-step authentication, manage the apps that have access to your data, and see a lot of all the times that your account has been accessed.

2.2. Evernote desktop

The Evernote application is available for both Windows and Mac—while they look a bit different, they include all of the same features, and they're accessed in more or less the same way.

| Sidebar | Note list | Note editor |

There are three main sections in the Evernote window:

1. The **sidebar**, where you'll navigate between different collections of your notes.

39

2. The **note list**, where you can move between individual notes.
3. The **note editor**, where you can create and edits notes.

There are also toolbars at the top of the screen from which you can take a lot of common actions. Let's take a look at each of these sections in a bit more detail.

Sidebar

The sidebar allows you to view your notes in groups. For example, you can view the notes that are in a certain notebook (a collection of notes). You can also view all of the notes that are in a number of notebooks that are all in the same stack (a grouping of notebooks), giving you a higher-level view of your notes. You can also view all of the notes that you have, regardless of where they are, which becomes useful if you know that you created a note recently, but can't remember where you put it. You can view your notes by tags (as you can see below, I find this very useful for getting to specific recipes that I want). And finally, you can view your notes by the location where they were created, if you've tagged them with this information. I haven't found a productive way to use this, but I imagine that it could be invaluable to someone like a travel writer.

Note list

This panel is largely self-explanatory. If you've selected a notebook, stack, or tag, every note in that group will show up here. There are quite a few different views to play around with, but I prefer the snippet view, because it keeps the notes well-organized and shows the first line or two of the note, so you can get an idea of what it's about if you didn't title it very well (which often happens to me when I'm making notes on the run). The notes are displayed in chronological order, starting with the most recent, and the created date is prominently displayed—it would be a good idea to make use of this feature by scrolling to the bottom every once in a while to see the notes that you haven't dealt with.

Note editor

This is where you'll be doing most of the work in Evernote. When you click on a note in the list, it'll show up here, ready to be edited (if you create a new note, it'll also show up here). The simplicity of the note editor is one of the best things about it—just click where you want to type, and type away. Already saved the note? Doesn't matter. It's always in editable mode. Want to change the notebook that it's in? Just select the right notebook from the dropdown menu. Want to add tags? Just click in the tags bar and start tagging. You can make changes to formatting, add attachments, share the note via social networking sites, and setup reminders (more on these later). It's amazing how much functionality is packed into this amazingly simple editor.

2.3. Evernote web

As I mentioned before, Evernote stores all of your notes on a central server—one of the advantages of this is that you can access them whenever you want, wherever you are. This is most easily done by using the web interface at www.evernote.com. After inputting your username and password, you'll see a copy of your entire Evernote database! (Unless you've created non-synchronized notebooks, of course.) From here, you can do all of the things that you can do from the desktop client. Create and edits notes and notebooks, manage stacks and tags, and so on.

The Evernote web interface.

43

Though the web interface looks a bit different than the desktop interface, it provides the same functionality— you'll recognize the sidebar, note list, and note editor that we discussed for the desktop version. It doesn't look quite as nice, but all of the important features are intact. You probably won't be using the web interface much, unless you often need to access your notes from a public computer, but it's nice to know that you always have the option.

2.4. Evernote mobile + Windows 8

One of my favorite parts of using Evernote—and certainly one that I find extremely useful—is the ability to access my notes while I'm on the go. I use Evernote on my phone and my iPad almost every day, whether it's to look up a recipe while I'm at the store, jot a quick note on the train reminding me to do something, or sketching out some work-related plans. And the fact that Evernote is completely cross-platform compatible means that I have no problem using it on my Mac, my Android phone, and my iPad.

To get started with Evernote on your mobile, you'll need an Evernote account; you should have one already from when you downloaded and installed the desktop version—if not, you can sign up for one when you download the mobile version. To install the app, just go to the app store (whether that's Apple's App Store, the Google Play Store, or the Windows Store) and search for "Evernote." You'll likely get a lot of results, as there are many add-on apps, but you can play with those later. For now, just select Evernote and install it (it's free).

Once it's installed, open it up, and you'll be asked for your username and password. Simply enter the details that you chose when set up your account the first time, and the app will connect to the note server, and in a few moments, you'll see all of your notes displayed on your screen. Very easy and very cool! Of course, if you haven't created any notes yet, you won't see much.

Obviously, the screen on a mobile device is much smaller than the screen on your laptop or desktop—because of this, not as much information is displayed in the home screen. All of the features are still there, but they're much more compact. How they're displayed differs a bit by the mobile OS that you're using, so I'll address them separately here.

Android

You'll notice that the home screen has a smaller version of the sidebar, from which you can create new notes, manage your notebooks and tags, and sync your device. The Quick Notes buttons are great, as they allow you to create new notes with text, audio, a photo, or an attachment on the fly without having to select a notebook first. This is incredibly convenient when you need to jot something down when you're out and about—you can just file it later.

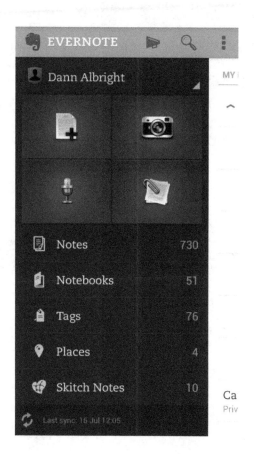

The Android home screen

By touching the notes, notebooks, or tags tab, you'll be brought to a browser screen for finding your notes based on one of those organization methods, letting you find the notes you need to get to with ease. You can also swipe from the right side of the screen toward the center to bring up the shortcuts menu, which is just like the desktop version; by adding notes, notebooks, or tags to this menu, you'll be able to access them very quickly whenever you need to. To add something to the shortcuts menu, simply touch and hold it from the appropriate viewing menu and tap Add to Shortcuts.

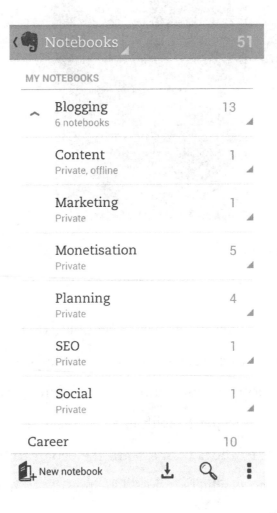

The Notebook list in Android Evernote

When you select a note, you'll be taken to the note screen, which allows you to use your entire screen to view and edit a note. When you first open a note, it's in view mode, so scrolling on the screen will allow you to move up and down through the note's contents, which is a great feature for when you just want to see what you've stored. To edit the note, tap the pencil icon in the lower menu bar, and you'll enter edit mode.

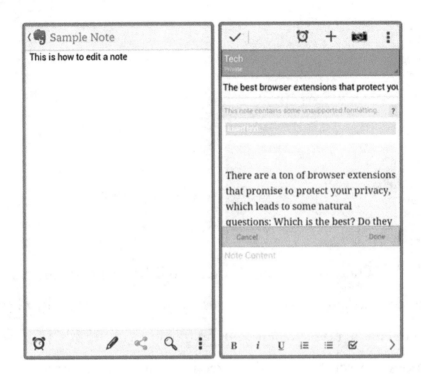

The note editing screen

From here, you can do everything you would from your computer—add and format text, attach photos and audio, set reminders, and delete the note. Although you can apply all sorts of formatting from here, I recommend just getting your text down and adding the formatting once you get back to your computer—it's a lot easier and will probably save you some time in the long run.

If you're going to be using Evernote on your iPhone or iPad, you'll get all of the same functionality, but the user interface looks a bit different. The tabs at the bottom of the screen allow you to view notes in different groups (all notes, notebooks, tags, and places), just like the desktop sidebar. The Quick Notes buttons allow you to quickly create new notes with text, audio, photo, or file attachments, saving you the time of selecting a new notebooks and hitting the + button near the top-right corner of the screen.

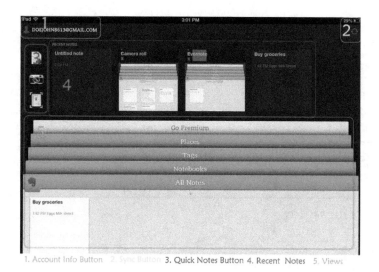

1. Account Info Button   2. Sync Button   3. Quick Notes Button 4. Recent Notes   5. Views

The iPad Evernote home screen.

On the iPad, recent notes are also displayed across the top of the screen, so you can resume working on something that you started earlier. By touching any of the organizational tabs at the bottom of the screen, you'll see a view that lets you navigate through your notebook library and select whichever note you need to.

The tags tab.

Once you've done this, you'll see the note screen.

Another nice organizational feature that the iPhone has is the ability to mark notes as favorites, allowing you to quickly access them from the Favorites notebook in the notebook view. This is very much like the shortcuts menu on Android. Once you've found the note you need, simply touch to open it.

When you first open a note, it'll be in the view mode, which allows you to see the note without the editing tools taking up valuable screen space. Simply tap the note to enter the editing mode. From the editor, you can do all of the things that you can do on your computer (edit, format, add text, add reminders, and so on).

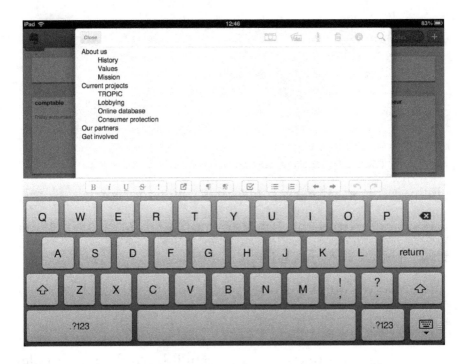

Editing a note on the iPad.

To save space, you can select "Simplified Formatting Tools," which will let you work with plain text, which is nice on the small iPhone screen. However, because of the larger screen size of the iPad, I like to work with the extended set of tools so that I can create notes with the same features as the ones I'd make on my laptop.

Windows 8

Evernote on Windows 8 looks quite a bit like Evernote on the iPad, though the navigational system is a bit different. When you open the app, you'll see a scrollable list of all of your notes (swipe to the left to scroll through). To navigate more precisely, swipe from the top of the screen towards the bottom to open the navigation bar, where you can access notebook and tag views. The menu bar on the bottom of the screen allows you to sort your notes, sync your account, and create new notes (this is available only when you're viewing the note list). And by swiping from the right side of the screen toward the center, you can search, share, and edit your settings. Once you've found the note you need, just tap to open it.

Like in the other mobile operating systems, the note first opens in the view mode, which allows you to read the contents of the note more easily. By touching the pencil icon, you can enter edit mode, in which you can add text and edit notes. As of this writing, Evernote for Windows 8 doesn't support rich-text formatting, so you'll have to stick with plain text and make any formatting changes you need when you get back to your computer.

All systems

There are a couple features that all of the systems have that I get a lot of use out of. First of all, Evernote includes a remarkably good search function, meaning that if you can remember anything about your note, you can probably find it relatively quickly by searching for some of the words in the title or the body of the note. Of course, if you *can't* remember anything about the note, or the contents of the note consist only of an image, this might not help much. But in most cases, it'll help you find a note quickly.

The other thing that I adore about Evernote mobile is the ability to share between apps. For example, on my iPad, I can use Wisdom Writer to compose a blog post or outline an article, and then import it into Evernote. This is valuable because Wisdom Writer is better for writing extended pieces. Similarly, you can send websites from Internet Explorer in Windows 8 directly to Evernote so you can check them out later. Take advantage of this!

2.5. Free or premium?

When you sign up for an Evernote account, you'll be asked at least a couple of times if you want a free account or a premium one. While this is totally up to you, I recommend you go with the premium version. Here's why:

1. Offline notebooks.

This is extremely useful. If you download notebooks to your mobile device, you can access them when you don't have internet access, which can be good when you're on a train or plane, if you're on the subway, or if you just don't have a good connection. If you stick with the free version, you'll need an internet connection to get your notes.

2. Increased protection.

You can add passcode protection to notes on your mobile, which makes it less likely that someone can get to your data if they nab your phone or tablet. While you might not be too worried about this right now, you might fall in love with the GTD-Evernote system, and start keeping everything in Evernote! While I wouldn't recommend storing credit card numbers or other sensitive financial information in a note, you might want to keep some things that you don't want other people to get access to. So protect them with a password.

3. Increased storage space.

Your monthly upload capacity is increased from 60 MB per month to 1 GB, which is a huge increase, and will be quite useful if you're going to be uploading just about every part of your life. If you're not sure whether or not you need a premium account, one way to figure it out is to use a free account until you start getting close to the 60 MB limit, and then upgrade so you don't have any problems with uploading additional content.

There are other advantages to a premium account, including the ability to search text within PDFs, better recognition of text in images, and more options when it comes to sharing and editing shared notebooks. Because the upgraded version only costs $45 per year (or $5 per month), I recommend going with a premium account. It's an incredibly valuable service, and it's a more than reasonable price for it. Plus, you're supporting the existence and further development of Evernote, which is a great thing to do for a company that offers such a fantastic product for free.

2.6. How does Evernote fit into GTD?

I hope it's becoming clear how helpful Evernote is going to be in your GTD system. However, just in case you're not quite seeing the whole picture yet, I'm going to lay it out here. In the traditional GTD system, you have a lot of trays and files in your office that serve to hold items (mostly documents of some sort) and keep them from getting mixed up. Things start out in the inbox, and then get dealt with, delegated, deferred, filed, or trashed. Evernote can play a role in all of these phases (though it's most useful in filing and tracking items through the various stages).

First, it can serve as an inbox. By creating a task

management system in Evernote (see the next chapter for more details), you can create a staging area that serves the same purpose as an inbox on your desk—things go there first, and then you decide what to do with them. Remember the questions from chapter 2: what is it? What's the next step? And do, defer, or delegate? Once an items hits your inbox—which is actually a notebook—you'll figure out what it is and what the next step is. Once you've done that, it'll be moved to the appropriate place so that it can be efficiently dealt with, either now or in the future.

Second—and this is where Evernote truly shines—it serves as an easily searchable filing system for everything that you want to keep filed for future reference. Because Evernote provides effective search functionality, finding whatever it is you're looking for is a breeze, even if you only remember a little bit about it. Let's say one of the things that you kept filed was a menu from the Chinese take-out place down the street (this is a great example of something that doesn't require any action, but might be useful later). You can remember that it's filed under the "Restaurants" notebook, or the "Chinese" tag, but you can also just search for "Chinese menu," and you'll likely find it. The original

GTD system used a physical filing system that would require you to keep it all in order and have at least a good idea of where to look for filed information. Evernote makes that exponentially easier and more effective, and you're much less likely to get overloaded. You can create up to 250 notebooks and 100,000 notes in Evernote. Can you imagine having 250 files full of 100,000 pieces of paper? It's a nightmare. This is much easier.

And this brings me to the third part—the trash. Sure, you can just delete things when they're done, or when they're no longer useful. But you can also use Evernote as an archive so that you won't lose anything. You may be tempted to trash a memo that you delegated and that was immediately dealt with, but just in case someone asks you about it later, you could just pull it up from Evernote to show them exactly when you received and delegated it. This is a bit of a contrived example, but you see my point.

4. Quick Setup in 1 Day

Want to get started right away? This chapter is for you. It'll show you how to download and install Evernote, help you get your first batch of items and tasks in order, and get your filing hierarchy setup

4.1. Installing Evernote

Because Evernote is such a popular piece of software, it's decently likely that you already have a copy of it on one of your devices. If you do, you can skip this section (though I do recommend downloading it on all of your devices, including your tablet and your phone). Fortunately, installing Evernote on a Mac, Windows, iOS, and Android is quite simple. We'll go in order.

1. Installing Evernote on a Mac.

First, go to www.evernote.com. You'll see a button on the homepage that says "Get Evernote—it's free." Click this button, and the download should start immediately. Once the download has completed, click on the disk image that's now in your Downloads folder to open it. Drag the Evernote icon to the Applications folder icon, and you're done. Double-click the icon in the Applications folder and launch it.

2. Installing Evernote on Windows.

Just like with a Mac, start by going to www.evernote.com and clicking the "Get Evernote" button. A download will start—once it's done, open the .exe file that just downloaded and follow the instructions to install the program.

3. Installing Evernote on iOS.

If you've ever downloaded an app on iOS, you already know how to get Evernote. Simply open up the App Store and search for "Evernote." It should come up right away—click Install and it'll start downloading. Once it's downloaded, open it up and enter the password that you chose on your desktop (you'll use the same username and password on all of your devices). You're all set!

4. Installing Evernote on Android.

Android is just as simple as iOS. Open the Google Play Store and search for "Evernote." Hit Install to download it, and once it's been downloaded, sign in. And that's it.

5. Installing Evernote on Windows 8.

Go to the Windows Store (either on your desktop

computer or mobile device) and search for "Evernote." You'll need to click or touch the "install" button to install the app on your device.

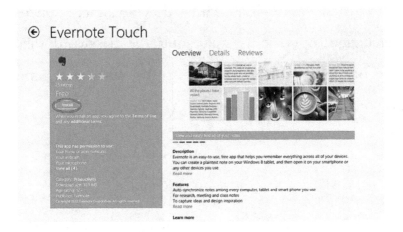

4.2. Notebooks and stacks

When you first install Evernote, there's not a whole lot there—in fact, there's just one notebook, and it's called "[your name]'s notebook," and it contains a single note called "Getting Started."

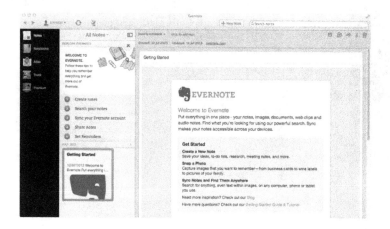

So what we're going to do is lay some of the groundwork for the successful implementation of the GTD system in Evernote. First, we'll rename your notebook (this is a great skill to learn early on). Click on "Notebooks" in the sidebar to switch to the notebook view. Click on the Notebooks tabs in the left panel. Right-click (or hold the control key while left-clicking) on your notebook, and select Rename Notebook.

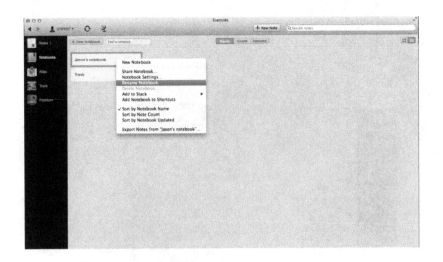

Change the name to Inbox. You may remember that this is a very important category of items in GTD, so it's fitting that it's your first notebook. You can imagine that Evernote notebooks are like files—they're containers for a specific kind of thing. Now, click the "New Notebook" button found near the top of the screen. Name this notebook Next Actions.

Now we'll create a stack, which is like a drawer: it's a collection of notebooks, or files, that can contain a number of types of things that are grouped together either by purpose or by the time in which they need to get done. Create another notebook called "Home." Then right-click (or control-click) on Home, and select Add to Stack -> New

Stack. Right-click on the new stack and name it Reference.

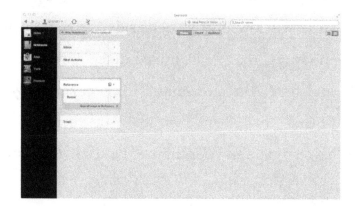

You can now add other notebooks to the Reference stack, so they'll all be kept in the same place. You could have "Home," "School," and "Work," or you could have "Lisa," "Haden," and "Jenn," or whatever you want. However you'd like to keep your items organized, you can do it with notebooks and stacks.

And that's basically all you need to know about notebooks and stacks! There are certainly other things that can be done with them, but these are the basic actions that you need: creating, renaming, and a bit of organizing.

4.3. Notes

Now let's create a note. Double-click on your Inbox notebook to open it and click "New Note in Inbox" (it's near the top of the window on the right side). It starts with no text in the body and the title "Untitled note." Just click in the title field and type "Buy groceries." Click in the body field and type "eggs," "milk," and "bread." And there you go— now you have an item in your inbox! It's ready to be moved through the GTD workflow.

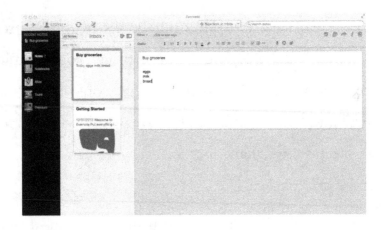

What is it? A grocery list. Is it actionable? Yes. When should it be acted upon? Friday. Make a note on your calendar (or use the Evernote reminder function, discussed later), and this can be moved out of your inbox. Easy. Let's say you don't have to buy groceries on a certain day, but you know you have to buy them soon. The Next Actions notebook would be a good place for this note.

You'll see that at the very top of the note editor, on the left side (to the left of the tags bar), the word "Inbox" is displayed with a little downward-pointing arrow next to it. Just click "Inbox" and then click "Next Actions" and your note will be transferred to that notebook. Couldn't be easier! (You can also right-click on the note in the note list and use the "Move to notebook" menu.)

Now let's delete that note. Click on "Notebooks" in the sidebar and double-click on "Next Actions." Open up the Buy groceries note. In the top-right corner of the screen, you'll see a garbage can. Click that and the note will be moved to the trash. Now let's say you deleted the note on accident—click on Notebooks, double-click on Trash, and you'll see your note is still there. You can empty the trash, but I wouldn't do it too often. It's nice knowing that your deleted notes stick around a while.

In the next two sections, I'll provide two different

systems that can be used to get your system set up here. Which you choose depends partly on the degree of organization that you're looking for, and partly on what you're using the GTD system to do. The first style is more complex, and it's great for those of us who use Evernote for just about everything in our lives. The second method is simpler, but still extremely effective. I recommend reading through the descriptions of both systems and deciding which one you think will be better for you.

4.3. System 1: tags

Once you have your notebooks set up, you're ready to get into the nitty-gritty of your Evernote organizational system: tags. Tags are like labels on your notebooks. If stacks are cabinets, and notebooks are drawers in those cabinets, then tags are the individual file folders. The advantage of doing this in Evernote, however, is that you never run out of room in a file! If you've ever tried to use a tagging system in a piece of software before, you might be a bit wary of this, and I understand your hesitation. It's really easy to start up an amazing tagging system and then lose track of it and have it all crash and burn after a few months. But with GTD, it's different—the tags are no longer just a labelling system. They act like a funnel. You'll see what I mean in a few moments. First, let's get your tags set up.

1. Create the upper-level tags.

In the Tags pane, click "New tag" and enter ".What". Don't forget the period at the beginning of the word—that's not a typo. Then add ".When," ".Where," and ".Who". These are your highest-level tags, and will serve to organize all of the others.

2. Create lower-level tags.

Now, you'll be creating a number of other tags. I've included a list below. Take a moment and create each one now (don't forget the punctuation):

.Active projects

.Inactive projects

!Daily

1-Now

2-Next

3-Soon

4-Later

5-Someday

6-Waiting

@Home

@Town

@Work

Also, create two or three tags with people's names (your spouse, a couple colleagues, your kids, whoever you're likely to have items on the list related to). In the Tags pane, you now have what looks like a big mess. However, Evernote provides the handy functionality of being able to nest tags. To see what I mean, click the ".Active projects" tag and drag it on top of the .What tag and let go. You'll see that ".Active projects" is now displayed below .Hey presto! How cool is that? Keep going, putting places under .Where and people under .Who, until you get something that looks like this (with your own tags, of course):

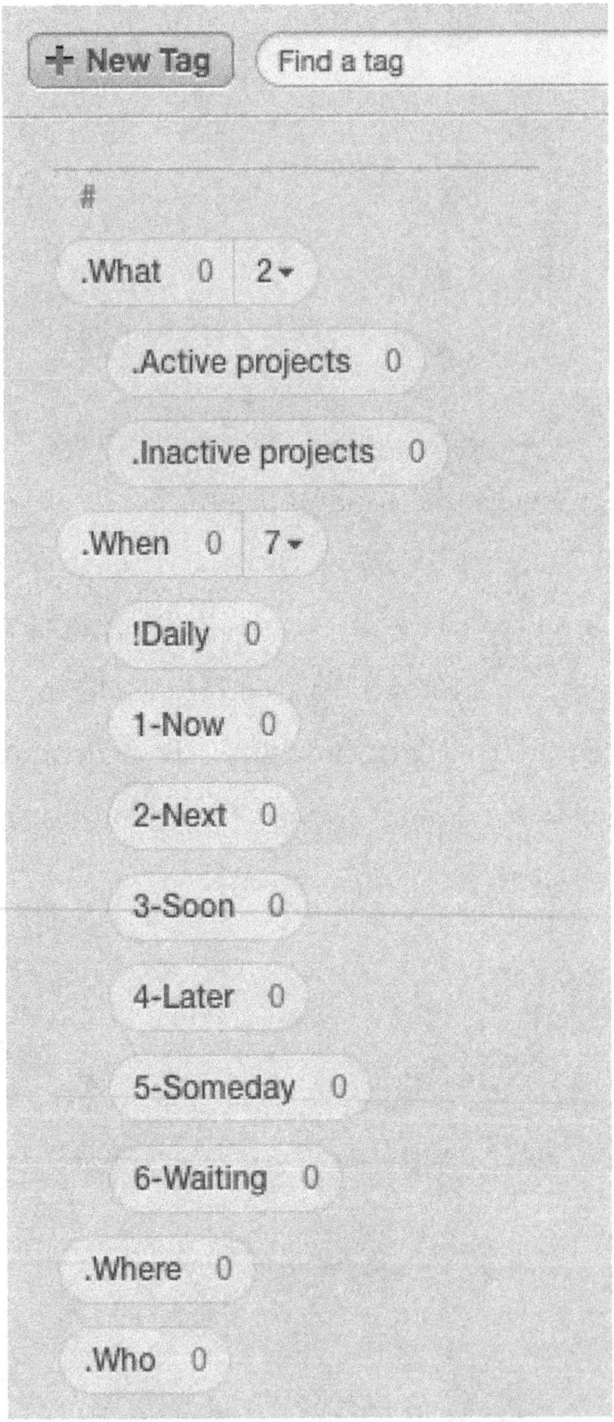

\#

.What   0   2▾

　　.Active projects   0

　　.Inactive projects   0

.When   0   7▾

　　!Daily   0

　　1-Now   0

　　2-Next   0

　　3-Soon   0

　　4-Later   0

　　5-Someday   0

　　6-Waiting   0

.Where   0

.Who   0

3. Lay the framework for your general reference filing system.

In the previous section, you created a stack for your general reference filing, and now it's time to flesh that out a bit. Right now, you have a notebook in there called "Home," but that's not going to cut it. This is where you get to customize the setup a bit. What kinds of things are you going to keep in your general reference system? Recipes? Create a notebook called "Recipes" and add it to the stack. How about receipts? Add that to the stack, too. Going to keep newsletters? Add it. Whatever you're going to keep in your general reference material should have a notebook. Don't be afraid to create a huge number of notebooks for this stack— the more clearly things are labelled, the easier they're going to be find later. Fortunately, tags and searching will help you find just about everything in a matter of seconds, but you might want to browse occasionally, and having a lot of accurately labelled notebooks is going to help that process. If you're looking for some examples, here are a few of the notebooks that are in my personal Evernote application:

- Class notes
- Dissertation
- Blogging
- Gift ideas
- Technology
- Saving money

Of course, I have loads more, and some of these are actually entire categories of notebooks (like Class notes; I probably have a dozen different notebooks labelled with the name of the course). Go crazy here! And remember that it's easy to rename a notebook, so if you decide to combine two notebooks or split one, you can easily give it another more applicable name.

4. Begin inbox management.

Your inbox, whether it's an electronic one, a paper one, or—more likely—both, can be managed wholly through

Evernote. Once the infrastructure for your system is in place, you're ready to start. It's time to start getting everything into your inbox.

First, gather all of the paper items from around your house or your office and put them in your physical inbox. Not just most things, or all of the things from your desk, but absolutely everything that's going to need to be dealt with at some time or another. It's much better to go all-out than to miss something!

Second, perform the "brain dump" that I mentioned earlier. Try to think of as many projects, tasks, and ideas that you have stored in memory and jot them down (in his book, Allen recommends writing each one on a single sheet of paper, but you can just create a new note in your Inbox notebook, which is much more efficient and environmentally friendly). As you go through the day, you'll start to remember more of these things—get them down immediately! Don't give yourself a chance to forget anything. This is a difficult step, but it's crucial. If something is in your head, it can be forgotten. If it's in Evernote, it's there forever. Think of as many things as you possibly can.

By the end of these two steps, your Inbox notebook and your physical inbox should be packed. Unfortunately, you're going to be adding a third inbox: the one in your e-mail account. Your e-mail inbox is likely going to be the most significant source of input into your GTD system, so it's good to integrate it into the system right away.

Okay, take a deep breath. It's time to start processing it all. This may seem like a monumental task, but using GTD and Evernote is amazingly effective. I recommend starting with your e-mail inbox, because it's likely causing you the most stress.

Many people feel overwhelmed when they start this process and don't know where to start. To make things easy, just start at the top, with your most recent e-mail (focusing on a single item at a time is a hallmark of GTD). Then just start going through the first couple questions of the workflow. What is it? Is it actionable? If not, should it be deleted? If yes, delete it and move onto the next list.

Should it go to the Someday list? If so, make a new note in Evernote, record the important contents of the e-mail (copy and paste will speed up this process), tag it with 5-

Someday, then archive the e-mail in your e-mail client. If it should go into general reference, make a new note in the proper notebook, enter the contents of the e-mail, and then either delete or archive the e-mail. If it's actionable, you can do it within two minutes, add it to a project, defer it, or delegate it. To add it to a project or list, just put the contents of the e-mail into a note and archive the e-mail. You can also institute a smaller GTD system in your e-mail inbox if that helps.

Let's look at some things you might have to do with a note that you created with the contents or action items from an e-mail. Does it need to be done around a certain time? Tag it with a .When tag for when it needs to be addressed. Is it an e-mail from your boss requesting a report? Better tag that with 1-Now. Is it from a colleague, reminding you that you need to get ready for a presentation next month? You can probably put that into 2-Soon. Did you get an e-mail about a service that you'd like to try, either at work or at home, but you're not quite ready to commit to paying for it? 5-Someday is a perfect tag for something like that. Every e-mail either gets a .When tag or can be immediately archived in your reference system.

In addition to adding .When tags, you should also be thinking about .What and .Who tags. Get an e-mail from your spouse? Tag it with her name. Copied on a conversation between several co-workers? Attach each of their names to it. Do you get messages about sales, marketing, social media, and sustainability for your company? Those can all be different .What tags. Fortunately, with Evernote it's easy to add new tags from within each item (just click in the tags bar and start typing), so you can create new tags on the fly.

Your use of .Where tags depends a lot on the kind of inboxes that you're managing—if you're only using this for work, you probably don't need to worry about them. But if you're going to be using GTD to manage your entire life (which I recommend), you'll want to use at least a few .Where tags to keep things straight.

While it'd be great to get your e-mail inbox completely cleared out in the first day, I know that's not always an option. So just start with 50 or 100 on the first day (I know it sounds like a lot, but once you get into the flow, it'll fly by).

So, now that you've cleared a good chunk of messages from your inbox, you should be seeing the value of this system—it didn't take nearly as long as you thought, did it?

5. Continue with your paper inbox.

Although we all *try* to be paperless, it's almost impossible to not have a paper inbox that contains things that need your attention. So what do you do about the things in there? You can't just add tags to them . . . or can you? In GTD, David Allen recommends creating files and using post-it notes or a labeller to essentially perform the same function as the notebooks and tags of Evernote. This is one possibility. You could have a few different trays on your desk, each of which contains one or more .When tags, allowing you to review them on the same schedule as you review your Evernote tags.

However, I prefer to go a different route (partly because my desk is already a mess, and adding more trays and organizational items might do more harm than good). In my experience, almost every piece of paper that hits your inbox can be dealt with in one of two ways. First, you can deal with it, because it takes less than two minutes. There are a lot of things that just need a signature or a quick look-over before filing. Process these right away and send them back on their way, either to whoever needs them next, or to your reference system.

The other types of paper items that are very common are those that require an electronic response. For example, I often get proposals and draft articles on my desk, and all that's needed is some feedback that I can give via e-mail. In this case, I add a new item to Evernote, call it something like "E-mail Jenny with article feedback," and add the piece of paper to a tray that I have for things that need to be reviewed. This tray used to get packed full of paper, and I rarely cleared it out, but now that I have a reminder for me to deal with a specific item, I do it as soon as I get the chance, and then remove the paper from the tray. Easy, clean, efficient.

I also find that a lot of the items that come to me in paper form are things that I want to keep, but that would be just fine as a scanned PDF. I have an app on my iPad called Tiny Scan Pro that lets me create quick, relatively high-quality scans with the camera—I snap a picture of both sides, import it into Evernote, and toss the paper (of course, this wouldn't work for a 50-page document, but 5 pages or so goes fairly quickly).

6. Begin dealing with items.

Okay—you've gotten started on the way to getting your inboxes under control. This is a quick-start guide, so you don't need to worry about getting your inboxes to empty (that'll take a while, but it's definitely doable, and should be one of your goals!)—instead, now it's time to start dealing with the things that you've processed and tagged. Here's a useful tip: start with the 1-Now items and do the worst one first; by doing the thing that you want to do the least, you'll feel accomplished, and you'll be well on your way to getting a lot done. Continue working through the 1-Now items. Once you finish those, move onto the 2-Soon items. If you're like me, it'll take you several days to get through the first round of 1-Now items, but once you get the system in place and running, you'll be able to keep that list quite small.

This is the end of the 1-day setup. You haven't

cleaned out all of the clutter yet, but you're well on your way, and you've put a system in place that will help you get there. To find out what to do next, read chapter 6, "Full Implementation in 7 Days".

4.4. System 2: notebooks

The second system that I'll detail uses notebooks and stacks instead of tags, and might be better suited to an implementation of GTD in which you're using your e-mail client to manage your electronic inbox (if you don't get hundreds of e-mails a day, for example, or if your e-mail client has superior labelling functionality, like Gmail). For simplicity's sake, I'll be referring throughout the rest of this book to the previous system, but if you decide to go with this one, it's easy to apply all of the following sections to this method. All of the steps are the same, but wherever I mention tags, you'll need to think about notebooks. Here's the setup that's used for this method:

1. Inbox*

2. Next Actions*

3. Projects**

—Project 1*

—Project 2*

...

4. Support materials**

—Topic 1*

—Topic 2*

...

5. Reference**

—File 1*

—File 2*

...

6. Someday*

*Notebook

**Notebook stack

As you can see, this system is much simpler. It is, in some ways, also more intuitive, as each grouping is self-contained and the items that are put into a certain stage are all kept together. It doesn't provide quite as much flexibility or detail, but the trade-off is that it doesn't take quite as much effort to maintain. As I mentioned before, this system might be better if you feel comfortable with using your e-mail client to manage your e-mail, if you just don't have to deal with very much e-mail, or if you're only using this to manage your personal life.

Of course, you can always expand this system by using some of the tags that were discussed in the previous section. In that way, this particular configuration is quite scalable, which is convenient. For example, you could change the "Next Actions" notebook to a "Tasks" notebook and use the 1-Now, 2-Next, 3-Soon, and 4-Later tags to keep track of the order in which you need to tackle these items. What it all comes down to is what you think will work best for you.

The nice thing about using Evernote to implement GTD is that you can combine methods that others have developed to create a system that will meet your needs. The setup that I use in my own personal management is a combination of several different systems along with some personal touches that fit my particular needs (for example, I occasionally do some freelance work, so I've created a Contracts notebook stack that contains a notebook for each contract that I take on—each notebook contains items related to that particular project). Don't be afraid to experiment and make adaptations!

Once you've set up the notebook hierarchy shown above, you can start with the process from the previous section at step 3 and follow the instructions from there (just use your notebooks instead of tags).

5. Tips for Immediate Benefit

I know a few people who have used Evernote for a while, not liked it much, but then come back to it and like it a lot more. What changes? First of all, they use it more. This is one of the crucial ways to make sure you get the most out of Evernote. The more you use it, the more it will do for you. When you have hundreds and hundreds of notes, the search and tagging functions will become invaluable, and you'll be amazed at how easy it is to find information whenever you want. It'll turn your computer into an encyclopedia of useful things you've come across—it's incredibly impressive when you think about it! I highly recommend incorporating it into as many parts of your life as possible.

Another way to make sure that you get the most out of Evernote is to use it on your mobile devices. Just about everybody has a smartphone now, and many people also have tablets—if you have the application with you wherever you are, you'll be able to jot down notes quickly so that you're reminded of things that you came up with on the run when you get back to your desktop or laptop. Although I like the idea of getting notes directly into the notebooks where they belong, you might want to create a notebook called "Mobile," in which you save all of the notes you create from your phone or tablet. If you do this, you can go back to those notes later to address any formatting issues and add additional information that you weren't able to capture on the fly.

6. Full Implementation in 7 Days

Now that you've gotten set up using your chosen system, and you've probably been using it for a couple days, you're likely looking forward to getting the entire system up and running. Fortunately, once you've completed the "Quick setup in 1 day" chapter, there's not all that much left. Most of what you'll need to do is actually in how you deal with the lists that you created and getting in the habit of working through things in the right order. In order to help you get everything working smoothly, I've given you seven tips here: one for each day of the week. I recommend starting this list on a Monday, as it'll help you get in the habit of conducting a weekly review on Monday morning, which is one of the most useful parts of GTD.

Monday: the weekly review

Every Monday, it's a very good idea to review outstanding items for the week ahead. Set aside at least 30 minutes to do this; I know that seems like a lot, and that you always have a lot to do on Monday morning, but trust me— it'll make the entire week more efficient. First, look at your calendar for the week, so that you're reminded of any day-specific items that are coming up: meetings, appointments, crucial tasks, and anything else that's tied to a specific day.

After that, look through all of the items that you've tagged with a .When tag (which should be anything that's currently incomplete—this can be a *very* long list) and see if it's still in the right category. For example, "Call Jerry" might have been a 3-Soon item last week, but needs to be upgraded to 1-Now because Jerry's going on vacation next week. And if there's anything in 5-Someday or 6-Waiting that can be moved up, make sure to do that.

The weekly review is helpful for reminding you of what's coming up, but it's also the perfect time to remind yourself of some of your larger goals, which are often represented in the 5-Someday category. If you're using your e-mail client to manage your e-mail, you should make sure that your weekly review includes going through any e-mails that might have ended up there over the weekend or any outstanding items that you weren't able to process last week.

Tuesday: the daily review.

This is another good habit to get into quickly. The daily review is essentially an abbreviated version of the weekly review. You don't need to go over all of the categories; just look at your calendar for the day as well as the first two or three labels and look for any extra-high priority items. The daily review should help you plan out the first few hours of your day. Take care of the items that are on your calendar first, as they're time-sensitive, then move to the 1-Now items. Once you've made this your daily routine, you'll have just about mastered GTD!

Wednesday: get in the habit of checking created dates.

Every item in Evernote has certain meta-data attached to it. The title and tags are two that we've gone over so far, but there's another important one that I'd like to mention here: created date. Whenever you create a note, the date and time are recorded, letting you know exactly when you created the note. When you're skimming through your items, make a note to look at the created date. If you notice that one of your items has been waiting to be dealt with for a long time, it's time to admit that it's not getting done. So what can you do about that? One of the best ways is to make that item a project and split it up into smaller items. For example, if you had "Write sales report" as an item, you could start a new project and include items like "Ask Sean for Q2 sales figures," "See if Cheryl has Q4 forecast," and "Create graphs from sales data." This should make the task much easier to tackle, and it'll keep it from getting stuck in one of your categories.

Thursday: learn to delegate.

It's vitally important to realize that not everything that comes across your desk should be dealt with by you personally. There are some things that you just won't have time for, and there will certainly be items that other people are better equipped to deal with than you are. And when either of these is the case, you need to be honest with yourself. Our society places a huge value on always being busy, getting a huge amount done, and taking on as much as responsibility as possible. For the sake of your mental health, it's crucial to remember that you *can* pass tasks off to other people if there's a good reason for it. This is an important part of the system, because if you're trying to process and accomplish tasks that you aren't well-equipped to deal with, you're going to be moving much more slowly through your list than you should be. Don't be afraid to admit that you need help or that you're just not the person for a particular item.

Friday: remember that you can hire work out.

Both your time and your mental health have a value! Remember that paying to delegate things is often worth it. For example, if you have a big project on your list, something like "Write up new content for website," it may be a good idea to think about hiring this out. If you're getting far too stressed out about a specific project, your priorities have changed, or you now realize that one of your tasks is much larger than you originally thought, and you no longer have the time or mental energy to do it, you can always hire help. Many of the tasks that you'll have to deal with at work can be adequately handled by freelancers, and it's usually pretty easy to find one that's quite affordable. It can be tough to get into this habit, but once you do it and realize how much better you feel having a big item off your list, you'll see that it's definitely worth it!

Saturday: use the !Daily tag to help you learn new habits.

The !Daily tag can be used for a lot of things, and is often used for things like "Check in with Mary," "Write daily summary," or "Pull yesterday's analytics." However, you can also use it to help you get into new habits. For example, let's say you want to start checking your competitor's website for updates to keep an eye on the competition. Give this a !Daily tag, and you'll be reminded every day during your daily review that it's something you should do. This also works for personal items, too—you can get into the habit of taking a walk over your lunch break every day, getting up to stretch every hour, or texting your kids. Anything that you want to get in the habit of doing can be greatly helped by this strategy.

Sunday: don't forget the GTD basics.

Once you get Evernote up and running, you'll be well on your way to becoming a GTD master. However, you need to make sure to keep the basics of GTD in mind to ensure that your workflow process is still efficient, and that you're not using Evernote as a giant information dump. Print out a copy of the GTD workflow and keep it at your desk(s). Keep labelled trays on your desk. Do whatever you need to do to make sure that you remember the three most important steps: What is it? What's the next step? Do, defer, or delegate?

By following these 7 tips, you'll have a fully functional GTD system using Evernote in about a week. Of course, getting into the habit of using it correctly will take a bit longer than that, and tweaking the specifics will take even longer. But if you've created the system and committed to using it, congratulations! You are on your way to becoming more organized, more productive, and less stressed than ever.

So what's next? If you want, you can simply stop here. You now have a complete system up and running, and if it's working for you and you're happy with it, great! You can leave it as is. However, if you're interested in becoming an organization and productivity master, read the next two sections on advanced Evernote functionality and super-advanced tips to see how you can maximize the utility of this system. And no matter whether you decide to go on to these tips or not, don't forget the final chapter, Going Forward, which has a few final notes on how to keep your system running smoothly.

7. Advanced Evernote functionality

One of my favorite parts about Evernote is that while it's primarily a simple note editor and organizer, it also packs some great advanced functionality. Some of these functions can help you out a lot with implementing GTD and making some things that you're likely to be doing both easier and faster. I'll highlight four of these here, but if you do some exploring in the application and online, you'll probably find plenty more! And if you click on "Trunk" in the sidebar, you'll see some recommendations from the staff at Evernote.

Web clipper

This is definitely one of the things that I use the most with Evernote. The web clipper is a browser extension that lets you clip websites directly into notes in Evernote. I use this a lot with recipes—whenever I see something that I think I might like to make sometime, I just hit the button in the menu bar in Chrome and that recipe is instantly entered into a new note in whichever notebook I choose. You can use browser bookmarking for this, sure, but the fact that you can tag all of your recipes (I tag mine by the main ingredient, whether or not it's dairy-free, and whether or not it's vegetarian) and search them is really useful. It's nice to be able to access them offline, too. And, of course, you can also use this for anything else that you want. Want to keep a collection of articles on blogging together where you can browse them later? Just clip 'em. See a picture of a shirt you like, and don't want to forget to look for it next time you're at the mall? No problem. The possibilities are literally endless.

Using the Web Clipper to save an article

To get the web clipper, go to www.evernote.com/webclipper and hit the "Get Web Clipper for [your browser]" button. Then just follow the instructions.

Reminders

This is a relatively new feature of Evernote, and it's one that I think a lot of people using GTD will find invaluable. By adding a reminder to a note, you'll get a reminder on a specific date both within the app itself and by e-mail. Your calendar should be reminding you of the important day-specific things, but this can be very useful for things in the Someday category. Let's say you find out about a concert that you think you might want to go to, but tickets don't go on sale for another two months, so you don't have to decide quite yet if you're going to go or not. You can set a reminder on a note that will tell you to decide whether or not you should go to the concert—if you decide to, you can add "Buy tickets" on the day they go on sale. By using reminders this way, you can keep things that aren't strictly day-specific, or are just slightly lower-priority, off of your calendar without forgetting about them altogether.

Adding a reminder to a note is the easiest thing in the world. First, click on the clock icon near the top-right side of the note editor.

If you click "Add a Date," you'll be able to choose the date on which you'll receive an e-mail and in-app reminder.

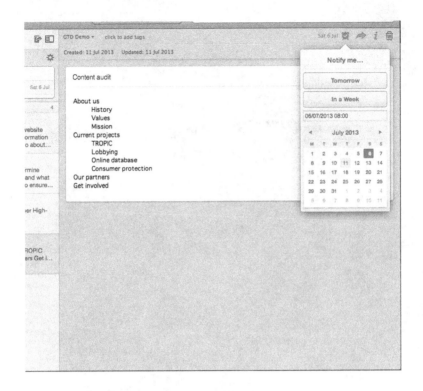

That's all there is to it! (Note: if you don't want to receive e-mail reminders, you can turn this off in the preferences window.)

Note linking

You've been able to add hyperlinks to your notes for a long time, which is great for keeping track of things that

108

include URLs, but you can now also create links to other notes, which can further help you organize your ideas. I like to use this in a series of documents if they don't have their own notebook.

Let's imagine that your colleague Janice has written up a bit of text for your website, and you've edited it. To keep track of this progress, you could go through the following steps. As you can see in the note list below, there's a memo from Janice and some updated site text. We're going to link the two notes together so that when you see Janice's memo you can see the updated text you wrote.

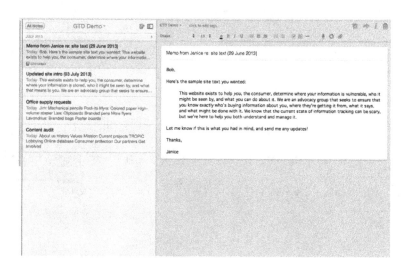

Once you've decided on the notes you're going to link, start in the note that you're going to add the link to, then right-click on the note that you'd like to create the link to.

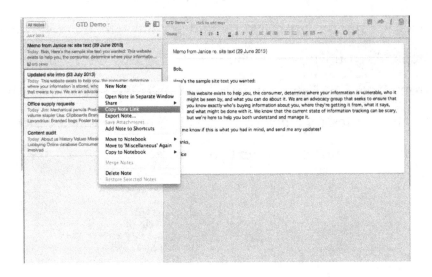

Select "Copy Note Link," and go back to the note that you want to create the link in. Click Edit -> Paste (or right-click and select Paste, or hit ctrl-V) to paste the link.

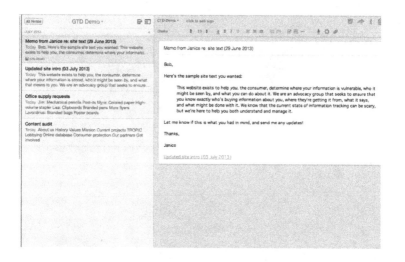

As you can see, there's now a link to the other note! All you have to do is click the link and the other note will open in the note editor. In this example, that's not that big of a deal, because they're right next to each other in the notebook, but if you have two notes that are in different notebooks, you can see how this would be useful. .

8. Super-Advanced Tips

If you've made it this far, you have Evernote set up and your GTD system is helping you manage your entire life. Most people will be more than happy to stop here—implementing all of this is quite a bit of work, after all. But some people either want or need to go to the next level, and this chapter is for you. I've included 5 additional tips here that you can use to further automate or add functionality to your system. Of course, you can pick and choose which ones you want to use—using them all would be overkill. But if you're a gadget geek like me, and this kind of thing makes you feel a little giddy inside, this is going to be a fun chapter, and it'll help you turn GTD-E into something that you'll enjoy even more!

We'll start with free things and go on from there.

1. IFTTT (If This, Then That).

This is an interesting service that links actions in accounts with other actions by using combinations called "recipes." For example, you can create a recipe that will send every Facebook status update from your account to your Twitter account, so that they're both updated at the same time. You can set up a recipe that will create a link on LinkedIn every time you publish a new blog with Blogger. You can also use the service to communicate things to you; for example, you can receive a text from the Weather Channel every morning letting you know what the forecast is for the day. By inserting Evernote triggers and actions in IFTTT, you can do things like have starred e-mails automatically imported from your Gmail account into Evernote, easily save Craigslist posts to Evernote, or archive your Instagram photos in a notebook. The possibilities are almost endless! Check it out at www.ifttt.com.

2. RSS clients and other readers.

There are a lot of useful apps out there for helping

you stay on top of things that you want to read. Two of my favorites are Feedly, an RSS reader, and Pocket, a document clipper. Both of these include integration with Evernote, so that you can store your favorite RSS items or clipped articles directly into a notebook. This means you can easily access them from anywhere that you're able to get into your account. While some of this functionality can be accomplished with the web clipper, it can be useful to have this set up if your personal system works better by keeping some things separated so you don't get inundated with information. While I only have experience with Feedly and Pocket, I know there are other apps like this out there that work directly with Evernote.

3. Camera apps.

While you can take photos directly from Evernote, other apps allow you some increased flexibility before importing the notes, either to edit them, or to reduce their size so they don't take up too much of your monthly upload capacity. For example, you can use FastEver Snap to take pictures and resize them before importing to Evernote. You can use an app like FotoNote to turn your images into electronic text before importing for easier reading later (this can be especially useful for things like receipts), or create photo memos with an app like Déjà Vu. There are a lot of possibilities here, and I encourage you to explore them! If you have a good camera or scanner app, you can go a long way toward being paperless much faster than you would have dreamed possible.

1. Moleskine Smart Notebook

Evernote has partnered with Moleskine to make a smart notebook that uses Evernote's Page Camera (on your tablet or phone) with specially designed pages and stickers to capture the notes that you write in the notebook and make them searchable. It's a really cool way to integrate analog and digital media! I haven't used this myself, but it's definitely on my list of have-to-try technologies. And it comes with a free three-month subscription to Evernote Premium, so you can try out the premium version before spending money on it if you'd like.

2. Doxie scanner

Doxie specializes in making small, portable scanners that you can take and use anywhere, even away from your computer. And it's integrated with Evernote, so you can bring it anywhere and scan whatever you want—receipts, tax forms, flyers, or anything else that you want to remember—and get it right away in Evernote. If you're looking to go totally paperless, this can be an incredibly helpful tool.

9. Going Forward

Congratulations! You've made it all the way to the end. You understand GTD, you know how to use Evernote to implement it, and you have a couple ideas for using the advanced functions in Evernote and the added capabilities you get from additional apps. You're a productivity master! There's honestly nothing left to do but make a couple notes here on things that you should keep in mind going into the future. So here are a couple closing thoughts.

1. Be ready for the unexpected.

I know that I spent the entire book telling you how to get everything organized and planned, but it's good to remember that life will throw you a curveball every once in a while. Fairly often, in fact. And it's good to be ready for these things. Every time something goes wrong in your system, or you discover something that doesn't quite work in every situation, make an adaptation that will help you deal with that issue next time. Of course, you'll be coming across new things all the time, so you won't ever be prepared for everything, but by continually adapting your system, you'll be better prepared to adjust to any new requirements.

To give you an example, I have a "Miscellaneous" notebook—and the idea of a miscellaneous notebook goes against most of the principles of GTD. However, I use it to keep things that are incomplete, that need more information before getting filed, or that need attention for some other reason. I check this notebook often, to make sure that the things in there get dealt with promptly. This is an adaptation that I've discovered that I need, because I often need to open a note quickly to jot down something while I'm on the phone, or copy down some directions, and I'm not quite fast enough to get it into the right notebook right away. Essentially, the "Miscellaneous" notebook is the equivalent of a desktop notepad.

2. Conduct a yearly review.

I've discussed the daily and weekly reviews, but there's one more kind of review you should be doing: the yearly review. This isn't quite like the others; you aren't going to be looking at your schedule for the next year to see what you have coming up. This is a time to review your overall priorities and get re-committed to whatever it is that you're trying to accomplish in your life.

It's also a good time to go through your general reference filing system and clean it out, if this is something you think you might like to do. I do it on occasion, but not very often—that's the beauty of Evernote. When the GTD book was released, the yearly review helped you keep your filing cabinets from overflowing all over your office. That isn't a problem anymore, but the idea is still a good one. If you think it might be useful, you can conduct a yearly review that includes more than Evernote—look at your bank accounts, your stock holdings, your mortgage . . . anything and everything you want to stay on top of, but doesn't require weekly or monthly attention.

And on that note, I wish you good luck with your organizational efforts. Stay committed to your system, and keep working to improve it, and it'll continue to make your life easier!

ABOUT DOMINIC WOLFF

Dominic Wolff is an author, business owner and traveller (or as he likes to call it, a globe trotter). A native from Idaho, Dominic became interested in the mechanics of business from a very young age. From those early days of selling candy bars to running a multi-state company today, Dominic has always been on the lookout for systems that would improve his productivity and allow him more free time to enjoy his hobbies. He frequently writes articles about personal productivity for business publications.

He believes that having a structure in place for work and life can mean the difference between being in control and merely coping.

An avid collector of fine red wines, he also owns a small wine boutique stocking only the finest of Washington, Oregon and Idaho wines. During his travels to far and wonderful places he also searches for the absolute best Zinfandel that can rival those of California. He lives in Wyoming with his wife Sarah, two German Shepherds and a tiny vineyard of his own.

BOOKS BY DOMINIC WOLFF

Getting Things Done (GTD) + Evernote = Ultimate Productivity

Total Time Mastery with Evernote

Your Killer Linkedin Profile

Building Connections 2014

Before You Start...

Thank you so much for reading my book. I hope you really liked it. As you probably know, many people look at the reviews on Amazon before they decide to purchase a book. If you liked the book, could you please take a minute to leave a review with your feedback? 60 seconds is all I'm asking for, and it would mean the world to me.

Dominic Wolff

CPSIA information can be obtained
at www.ICGtesting.com
Printed in the USA
LVHW080802030123
736285LV00006B/262

9 780990 422105